With Love

To Chris & Terry

From Dave & Sandy

Christmas 1996

The corporate seal of the city of Joplin, adopted January 30, 1917, with the motto, "Zinc Is King." On display at the city of Joplin Municipal Building.

JOPLIN

A PICTORIAL HISTORY

by Kay Kirkman and Roger Stinnett

Design by Jamie Backus Raynor
Donning Company/Publishers
Norfolk/Virginia Beach

Library of Congress Cataloging in Publication Data:

Kirkman, Kay, 1935-
   Joplin, a pictorial history.

   Includes index.
   1. Joplin, Mo.—Description. 2. Joplin, Mo.—History.
I. Stinnett, Roger, 1942-   joint author. II. Title.
F474.J8K57   977.8'72   80-20530
ISBN 0-89865-070-4 (pbk.)
Printed in the United States of America.

This is a representative of the wagons of miners who headed for Joplin when lead was discovered. Taken in 1912, the photograph was one of several used as models by Thomas Hart Benton when he created the mural for Joplin's Centennial celebration. From the Dorothea B. Hoover Historical Museum

Contents

The Joplin Union Depot was designed by Louis Curtiss, a nationally famous architect who pioneered in metal and glass curtain wall building, and reinforced concrete construction. The station was opened by a cheering crowd on July 1, 1911, when a Missouri, Kansas, and Texas Railroad train arrived at 10:30 p.m. The depot was placed on the National Register of Historic Places in 1972. Currently, efforts are underway to restore the building for commercial use. From the postcard collection of Ron Mosbaugh

Thomas Hart Benton painted his only autobiographical mural in honor of the 1973 Centennial of the city of Joplin, Missouri. Benton's last signed and completed mural reflects his memories of early mining operations in Joplin and the beginning of his art career in 1906 as a seventeen-year-old newspaper cartoonist on the Joplin American. The Joplin Council for the Arts commissioned the mural at a cost of $60,000 for the lobby of the Joplin Municipal Building. A $10,000 matching grant from the National Endowment for the Arts program of Works of Art in Public Places seeded the project and was matched by the City Council of Joplin. The remaining amount was raised by voluntary contributions which included $1,000 from the students of Joplin's public schools. All reproduction of the Benton mural is protected by the Joplin Council for the Arts, the copyright owner. © 1972.

Preface

A newcomer to Joplin would see a middle-size city of some 40,000 people, a profusion of trees on the gently rolling streets, a downtown section more attractive than many, obviously refurbished. Joplin has the usual shopping malls scattered through town, a street lined with motels and fast-food restaurants, many beautiful old homes, and several new housing additions. There are two colleges, three hospitals, and more than one hundred churches. Joplin looks like a peaceful town, one of those nice, middle American towns whose virtues are extolled by writers and politicians. It occupies little space in the history books, and if someone mentions that Joplin is the town that jack built, the newcomer will probably wonder for a moment who "Jack" was.

But jack was a mineral, not a person. And the discovery of jack in the late 1800s helped to turn Joplin into a booming, violent city with a reputation as a "sin city," a notoriety which lasted well into the next century. Fortunes could be made practically overnight by a man with a pick and shovel, a strong arm, and a little luck. The area was called the "Klondike of Missouri," and produced more wealth than the gold fields of the Klondike in Canada. And with the wealth came the people who knew how to spend it.

This is the story of the city of Joplin, the town that jack built.

The Country of the Six Bulls

1800–1873

In 1803 the Louisiana Purchase more than doubled the size of the fledgling United States of America. Adventurers, traders, and trappers moved quickly to explore and exploit this vast new territory.

One such man was Edmund Jennings, who left his home in Tennessee, came to the southwest corner of what is now the state of Missouri, and lived with the Indians for about fifteen years in the early 1800s. The Osage roamed this area until the Emigrant Indians (Cherokee, Delaware, Wea, Kickapoo, Piankashaw, Shawnee, and Peoria) exchanged their lands east of the Mississippi for a home in the former land of the Osage.

The country was heavily wooded; game was abundant and water plentiful. Yet Jennings felt the urge to return to Tennessee. When he arrived, he was a stranger in his own land. It had been so long since he had spoken English, his friends could barely understand him. He tried to describe the place where he had been, and to pinpoint it, he said it was "the country of the six bulls." Or so his friends understood him, not realizing that Jennings was trying to say six *boils*—places where the water ran rapidly in a boiling manner. For many years, this misunderstanding caused the area where Joplin is now located to be called "The Country of the Six Bulls."

John C. Cox was intrigued by Jennings' account and that of Nathan Boone, son of Daniel Boone, who encouraged Cox to go west. In 1836 Cox came to this area and found the six "bulls" which are now called Cow Skin Creek, Indian Creek, Shoal Creek, Center Creek, Spring River, and North Fork. Cox was pleased with the land, and in 1838 he returned with his wife and sister, built a log cabin and a general store, and settled down.

He was not the only settler in "The Country of the Six Bulls." William Tingle from Delaware began farming northwest of Cox's home in 1837. Solomon Rothanbarger from Pennsylvania had homesteaded on Turkey Creek about the same time. It was Rothanbarger who would begin in 1842 to construct kilns which would provide building bricks for most of the new settlers' homes.

And in 1839, the Reverend Harris G. Joplin, a Methodist home missionary, settled beside a spring and built a log cabin large enough to hold church services. Soon the spring and creek into which it flowed were called by Joplin's name.

But the force which was to form the town called Joplin was concentrated in other areas. The mineral wealth which had been deposited here millions of years before was still hidden and waiting.

There is disagreement over who made the first discovery of galena (lead). Some say that Pete, a young Negro slave owned by Cox, uncovered the shiny, heavy rocks while digging for fishing worms. Others say that David Campbell, a miner from Washington County in eastern Missouri, recognized on Tingle's farm some depressions that

This is reputed to be a photograph of the Reverend Harris G. Joplin, for whom the city of Joplin was named. Born in Tennessee in 1810, he came to Jasper County around 1839 and organized the first Methodist congregation, which met in his small log cabin. According to a description related in The Story of Joplin *by Dolph Shaner, "He had a clear, well-trained voice, was highly excitable, deeply in earnest, and at times, grew most eloquent, holding his small audience spellbound. He was about 5'8" tall and weighed about 160 pounds . . . He was devoted, ambitious, and liberal to a fault, which caused him to become financially embarrassed, and made it necessary for him to dispose of his meagre belongings . . . At the earnest solicitation of his friends in Greene County [Missouri] he returned there, where he died in the fall of 1847 at the age of 37." From the Dorothea B. Hoover Historical Museum.*

13

The Rothanbarger residence, now known as History House, has changed very little since it was built on the original 1837 homestead of 380 acres. Clay for the bricks was taken from a clay pit on the grounds. The foundation was laid with the North Star for a compass, and the huge blocks of chiseled limestone have not shown a sag or a crack in more than one hundred years. All the rooms are approximately seventeen feet square, and the brick walls are between fifteen and seventeen inches thick throughout the house. Rafters are joined with wooden pegs, and nails used were square-headed wrought iron. The house has been beautifully preserved and is presently owned by Myral Butler. From the Dorothea B. Hoover Historical Museum.

indicated mineral deposits and dug out the first lead. However it happened, the small community uncovered one of the largest deposits of lead in the world.

Of course, no one realized at first how big it was. And the Civil War disrupted lives in this corner of Missouri as much as it did in Virginia or Pennsylvania. Cox's home was burned by bushwhackers, forcing him to take his family to Neosho for refuge. The bushwhackers tried to burn the Rothanbarger home, charring the kitchen and the rafters, but the house survived and was used by both sides as a first aid station for wounded soldiers.

When the war was over, life resumed at a quickened pace. Cox returned and rebuilt his house and store, increasing his trade with the growing number of new settlers.

In August 1870, E. R. Moffet and J. B. Sergeant leased from Cox about ten acres of land on Joplin Creek in order to sink a mining shaft. They were experienced miners, having just won $500 in a contest sponsored by the Granby Company at Oronogo, Missouri, for the miners who brought up the most lead from any shaft between March 4 and July 4. On the Cox land, the two miners struck a rich ore body that produced $64,000 in lead in the first ninety days. Like other area miners, they were disgusted to find the lead mixed with sphalerite (zinc), but they managed to separate the two minerals in the milling process, leaving behind piles of zinc, which they thought was worthless "jack."

On June 22, 1871, *The Carthage Banner* reported: "There is a new town in Jasper County. Its name is Joplin, and it is located fourteen miles southwest of Carthage on the farm of J. C. Cox. It has lead in unlimited quantities under it. Everybody out of employment ought to go there and dig. That is better than doing nothing and it may lead to a fortune."

The boom was underway.

Cox quickly platted a townsite of seventeen acres on the east side of Joplin Creek, naming it Joplin City as the new miners were calling it after his former neighbor.

Thirty-eight days later, another town sprang into being on the west side of the creek—Murphysburg. The rivalry between the two towns was intense. Cox moved the post office, which he ran, to Joplin City, strengthening its position. Patrick Murphy, the founder of Murphysburg, offered an additional building lot free to every buyer who would put up a store building or a residence on his side of the creek. Name-calling and rock-throwing quickly became elevated to fisticuffs and gunfights. As speculators grabbed land and mining companies fought for leases, gamblers, prostitutes, and various hoodlums joined in the fray. With the nearest law enforcement officer in Carthage and a tent city of more than 500, it's not surprising that

John C. Cox, the founder of Joplin, was born in Burke County, North Carolina, September 6, 1811. His family moved to Tennessee when he was eight, and he came to what is now Joplin in 1836. In June of 1838 Cox, his wife, and his sister returned to settle about one-half mile north of the existing house. He built a store of hewn logs and established a post office, where he served as unpaid postmaster for thirty years. One of the first discoveries of lead was made on his land as was the first mine shaft in the Joplin camp. Cox became wealthy from mine royalties. He platted Joplin City on July 28, 1871. Cox died January 23, 1890. *From* The Mines and the Miners; *courtesy of Bob Phillips*

This photograph of the Cox residence was taken in 1867. The house, which was called Wig Hill, is still standing and occupied by descendants of John Cox. From the State Historical Society of Missouri

by the beginning of 1872 Joplin was in the middle of what was called the "reign of terror," a time of almost open war.

People were frightened, and the leaders of the two towns realized that they must unite and provide some form of law enforcement. In March 1872 Joplin City, with a population of 1,364, and Murphysburg, with 1,343, merged as Union City, with J. W. Lupton immediately appointed to be marshal.

Although Lupton cooled the reign of terror, the town was still divided. The first bank, the National Savings Bank of Joplin, and the first hotel, Bateman House, opened on the east side. But the west side managed to get the post office transferred to them. Angry citizens petitioned the court to dissolve Union City, and Joplin City and Murphysburg became separate towns again. Union City had lasted just nine months.

The two towns needed each other, however. And so, one year later, Joplin received its city charter on March 23, 1873, and E. R. Moffet, one of the miners who sank the shaft that started the rush to Joplin, was appointed as the first mayor.

Now if they could just get rid of all those piles of jack.

This was the original building in which John Cox had his general store and post office. The building is gone now, but two of the logs as well as the desk which Cox used for the mail are preserved in the Dorothea B. Hoover Historical Museum. From the Dorothea B. Hoover Historical Museum

One of the partners who dug the first bonanza shaft in Joplin was J. B. Sergeant. A native of Indiana whose first lead mining experience was in Galena, Illinois, Sergeant met E. R. Moffet at Oronogo, Missouri, where the two earned a $500 prize for mining the most ore in a set period of time. Sergeant was active in many Joplin enterprises, including the establishment of the Joplin and Girard Railroad, the Joplin Railway Company, the Bank of Joplin, and the Joplin Flouring Mill. From The Mines and the Miners; courtesy of Bob Phillips

E. R. Moffet was born in Ohio in 1828. He went to California during the gold rush of 1849, to Texas in 1860, and in 1867 to Oronogo, Missouri, where he became a mining partner with J. B. Sergeant. Moffet's first house was a blanket stretched on four poles. After digging the Joplin Discovery Shaft which produced sixty thousand dollars worth of lead in the first ninety days, Moffet built a much more substantial residence. He was active in Joplin's business and political life, serving as its first mayor in 1873. He died in 1904. From The Mines and the Miners; courtesy of Bob Phillips

William Tingle was an early settler in the Joplin area. His farm at Leadville Hollow, two miles west of Joplin, was the scene of one of the first discoveries of lead in about 1848. Tingle and David Campbell, reputedly a nephew from Washington County, Missouri, dug out more than 100 pounds of lead from their first discovery and later opened other mines which were the best-paying in the county before the Civil War. From The Mines and the Miners; courtesy of Bob Phillips

Chapter 2

The Town that Jack Built

1873–1898

E.R. Moffett had a pretty good idea of what to do with the jack. He and several of his friends sent a carload on speculation to the smelter in LaSalle, Illinois. They were pleased to receive $5 for the carload, but even more pleased to learn that they could get as much as $15 for a carload of high grade jack, the stuff the miners around Joplin had been throwing away—the stuff, in fact, that was mixed with the piles of chat and gravel which were being used to macadamize the streets of Joplin.

It was fitting that the streets should be paved with some of the ore the miners were bringing up, since lead and zinc were being used for everything else in Joplin. In the fall of 1873 the rest of the United States was in the midst of a panic set off by railroad speculation combined with overexpansion in industry and agriculture. Money was hoarded and actually became unavailable in many places. But in Joplin, the mayor issued a proclamation saying that lead could be used for money, a practice that most merchants already allowed. In Joplin lead and zinc were as useful as gold. In fact, when the Joplin and Girard Railroad was completed on August 26, 1877, a lead spike rather than a gold one was used to complete the final link.

Most of the miners were paid on Saturday night, and the stores and banks stayed open late to accommodate them. The town was filled with people: families buying supplies for the week, friends and relations visiting, gamblers looking for an easy mark, prostitutes waiting for men with money. It was a rowdy, noise time, fueled by liquor from the many bars. One source lists seventy-five saloons in Joplin in 1875 when the population was about 5,000.

But other influences were beginning to appear. By the end of the 1870s, Presbyterian, Methodist, Catholic, Episcopal, Christian, and Baptist churches were established. The Congregationalists formed a nonsectarian society and built at Fourth and Virginia a tabernacle which became the center of activities ranging from revivals to roller skating.

Social groups were forming too. Joplin Lodge 287 of the Odd Fellows was formed in 1872, followed shortly by the Masonic Lodge, German Social and Literary Society, and the Knights of Pythias. In 1872 Peter Schnur started a weekly newspaper called *The Mining News*, which was succeeded by his *Joplin Daily News*. When the 1870s drew to a close, Joplin had a paid policeman, an opera house, a public cemetery (now known as Fairview Cemetery), a gas works for lighting, a theater, a library association, and a board of trade. The mining camp atmosphere was beginning to disappear.

By the time 1880 dawned, a writer for the Kansas City, Fort Scott and Memphis Railroad could say, "Many very good and very sensible

*This pen-and-ink sketch of the Joplin
Leadworks was first published in*
Historical and Descriptive View of
Missouri, *volume 1, which was
printed in 1891. From the State
Historical Society of Missouri*

people have come to think, and with good reason too, that mining communities are rough and disorderly and that most of the evils which curse society are openly tolerated. This estimate is often true. . . .but, happily, Joplin and the Joplin district do not labor under either of these disadvantages."

In fact, Joplin was trying so hard to overcome its rough and disorderly image that in 1878, when the great temperance revival known as the "Murphy Red Ribbon Movement" came to Joplin, 12,000 citizens signed the pledge. Since there were only 7,000 people living in Joplin at that time, it appears some of the citizens were trying too hard!

Joplin was fascinated with racing, whether between horses or men. Foot races were popular at a track northeast of the future site of the Union Station. A horse racing track with a straight, half-mile course was built south of the city in 1872. The Joplin Exposition in the late 1870s added a two-story art and floral hall mounted with an observatory, a grandstand for the races, and an amphitheater that seated 3,000. The park was later known as Barbee Park.

As Joplin became more settled, people had the time and felt the need for more recreational pleasures. The worries of the prolonged drought, arguments over free silver and protective tariffs, concern over the price of lead. . . .all could be forgotten at one of the galas planned by members of society.

The social event of the year was always the masked ball held at the Joplin Hotel on the corner of Fourth and Main. When the Schifferdecker Gardens opened on July 4, 1876, hundreds of people gathered for the celebration. The gardens featured a raised platform for dancing, bowling lanes cut in the meadow, and of course, good, cold beer brewed by Charles Schifferdecker himself from fresh spring water and kept chilled in the cave where the temperature stays below fifty degrees.

There were many German settlers in the early days of Joplin, including Schifferdecker, Ed Zelleken, Levi Riseling, John Roesch, Chris Guengerich, and Peter Schnur. In 1892 the Germania Society dedicated a hall on the southwest corner of Third and Joplin. Groups from Springfield, Carthage, Nevada, Fort Scott, Pittsburg, and Galena helped open the hall and enjoyed a dinner which included "cold turkey, chicken, beef, veal, mutton, ham, beef tongue, roast pork, goose and duck; potato, beet, radish, cabbage and celery salads; white, brown and rye bread; cheese of various kinds; cake; oranges, apples, bananas, grapes, coffee, tea and wine."

In 1888 Joplin held a special election which elevated it to a city of the third class. It was a surprisingly progressive town. The Sisters of Mercy had opened an academy in 1885 and founded St. John's Hospital in 1889. The first paid fire department was organized in

This bird's-eye view of Joplin, made
in 1877, shows chat piles extending to
the horizon. From the Joplin
Chamber of Commerce

Dr. J. C. Petit operated the Southwest
Medical and Surgical Institute on
Broadway in the 1870s. This natatorium was 14 by 35 feet and ranged
from 4 to 10 feet deep. Patients went
first to the Turkish baths and then to
the natatorium, which had a current
of fresh water running from a fountain
and "imparted a sense of refreshment
and vigor" as a result of a gentle
amount of electricity run through
the water from an electro-magnetic
battery. From the State Historical
Society of Missouri

1884, and Washington School and Joplin High School were centers for instructing the young people.

A telephone system was installed by C. W. Daniels in 1881, connecting Carthage, Carterville, Galena, Webb City, Oronogo, and Empire City, Kansas, with Joplin. The Joplin Water Works was built with a 1½ million-gallon capacity. The Joplin Brewery had been started by Muenning and Zontner. The Joplin Woolen Mill Company on south Main opposite the Missouri Pacific, Kansas City, Fort Scott and Gulf depot was two stories high and produced 500 yards of material per day.

The Joplin Flouring Mills of J. B. Sergeant had an elevator which held 40,000 bushels of wheat and ground 250–275 barrels of flour per day. John Klotz's Cigar Manufacturing Company at Main and Second was producing the Belle of Joplin along with Genuine Havana and First Trip. Sergeant's street railway had mules which drew cars called dinkies over the wooden rails. And the first electric light plant at 414 Joplin was bringing light, somewhat sporadically, to Joplin. Joplin was moving toward the new century full speed ahead!

Parades have been popular in Joplin since the town began. This photograph, circa 1880, shows the First Presbyterian Church, located on the northeast corner of Main and Seventh. From the Dorothea B. Hoover Historical Museum

The Keystone Bar was one of the many saloons that catered to the miners' thirst in the 1880s. From the Dorothea B. Hoover Historical Museum

This 1890s photograph shows the Terminal Bar and Joplin Hotel in the one hundred block of north Main on the west side of the street. (The hotel shown is not the original Joplin Hotel.) Some of these buildings are still standing. From the postcard collection of Ron Mosbaugh

One of the seventy-five bars that served Joplinites in the 1870s and 1880s. Notice the Anheuser Busch advertisements over the mirror. From the Dorothea B. Hoover Historical Museum

Interior of the Keystone Bar, which was located on the east side of Main, north of Fourth Street. From the postcard collection of Ron Mosbaugh

Sister Mother Mary Ignatius Walker led the group of twelve Sisters of Mercy who came to Joplin in 1885. She was instrumental in starting Our Lady of Mercy Academy. The Sisters of Mercy also started St. John's Hospital and contributed greatly to the development of Joplin. Courtesy of St. John's Medical Center

The Academy of Our Lady of Mercy was established by the Sisters of Mercy in 1885. The first Catholic school met in 1882 in a converted house with one teacher and seventy-eight students ranging in age from six to seventeen. The Southwest Missouri Regional Catholic School System now includes four buildings and over 500 students. From the State Historical Society of Missouri

HUTCHINSON & CO., PHOTO.

This photograph shows the interior of an early Joplin general store. Note the open boxes and barrels of food items. From the postcard collection of Ron Mosbaugh

The Wells Fargo and Company Express was located at 117 West Fourth when this photograph was taken in the 1890s. From the postcard collection of Ron Mosbaugh

This photograph of a Budweiser beer wagon drawn by oxen was taken in the 1880s in the 500 block of Virginia. Chickering Cement Company, shown to the right, was established in 1878 and remained in the Chickering family for three generations. The building was never wired for electricity because Chester L. Chickering said that if he couldn't make a living in the daylight, he'd quit! From the postcard collection of Ron Mosbaugh; courtesy of Chester L. and Helen Knight Chickering

The Reding and Clark Flour and Feed
Store was located in the 1300 block
of Main. Reding's Mill, on Shoal
Creek south of Joplin, had been a
landmark since 1832 when a wooden
dam was constructed on top of the
natural stone ledge and a set of
small burrs installed. Later, John S.
Reding twice replaced it with
successively larger mills. The final,
four-story mill, probably one of the
most photographed structures in the
Joplin area, was destroyed by fire in
1932. The Reding and Clark Flour
and Feed Store was torn down in the
1970s. From The Mines and the
Miners; courtesy of Bob Phillips

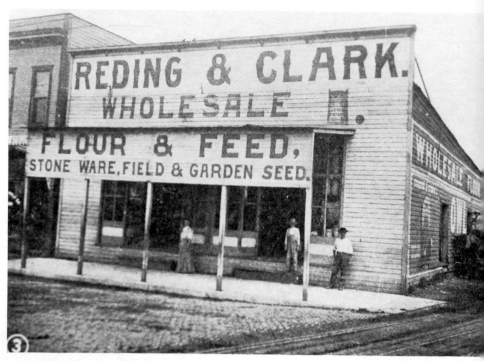

The shape of the racket and the style of clothes have changed since these Joplin residents enjoyed a game of tennis in the 1890s. From the Dorothea B. Hoover Historical Museum

Joplin High School was built in 1896 at the southeast corner of Fourth and Byers. The building had a long association with education in Joplin, becoming a junior high school in 1918 and a junior college in 1937. The building was finally razed in 1961. From the postcard collection of Ron Mosbaugh

6828. Joplin High School, Joplin, Mo.

This group of young people in 1888 formed the first high school class to graduate from Central School. The two-story, red brick building was located on Eighth between Joplin and Wall where Memorial Hall was later built. Central School was replaced in 1896 by Joplin High School. From the Dorothea B. Hoover Historical Museum

The Club Theater, built in 1891 at the southwest corner of Fourth and Joplin, was a popular place for dramatic and musical events around the turn of the century when this picture was taken. Along with the Haven Opera House on the northwest corner of Fourth and Virginia, the New Joplin Theater, and the Joplin Opera House on the northeast corner of Second and Main, the Club Theater attracted touring companies ranging from midget shows to Shakespearean plays. The Club Theater was destroyed by fire in 1918. From the State Historical Society of Missouri

The Keystone Hotel was built in 1892 at the southeast corner of Fourth and Main. The six-story building was constructed by E. Z. Wallower of pressed brick and stone at a cost of $100,000. Heated by steam, lighted by electricity and gas, it boasted the first elevator in Joplin. According to Woods Directory of 1895, "The commodious office, situated on the first floor, is the most popular resort in the city for capitalists, mine operators, and professional men. . . .Withal, making the Keystone Hotel the palace hotel of the Southwest." Courtesy of the Joplin Historical Society

Although the Jasper County seat is in Carthage, Missouri, Joplin had a courthouse for the Western District built on the southeast corner of Seventh and Virginia in 1894. The courthouse was completely destroyed in a spectacular fire on June 13, 1911. From the State Historical Society of Missouri

Music was an important part of every public celebration in Joplin. This photograph shows the band which played at the dedication of the courthouse in 1894. Courtesy of the Joplin Historical Society

St. John's Hospital was located at Twenty-Second and Ivy (now Connor). The hospital was the result of community effort fanned by Mother Mary Francis Sullivan and the other Sisters of Mercy. Patrick Murphy donated the land, and other funds were raised by businessmen and mine owners, as well as through a series of benefits, bazaars, and other entertainments. The Carthage-stone building cost $40,000 and was completely furnished with the best equipment of the day. St. John's Hospital was dedicated on October 4, 1900. From the State Historical Society of Missouri

Turnvereins, German exercise clubs, were very popular in the United States as a wave of interest in physical fitness swept through the country in the 1890s. In Joplin, the Germania Hall at the corner of Third and Joplin was the center of activity of all types as evidenced by this photograph of the German Turnverein Club Band with zithers. Courtesy of the Joplin Historical Society

These young ladies wore their finest, as did their horse and carriage, for an early Joplin parade. From the Dorothea B. Hoover Historical Museum

This 1896 photograph shows the Christman home at the corner of Ninth and Virginia. Bicycles were quite popular in Joplin around the turn of the century as witnessed by the fact that the Joplin Bicycle Club had 200 members. Courtesy of the Joplin Historical Society

The Joplin Hotel at the northwest corner of Fourth and Main was built by J. H. McCoy in 1875 and was the center of the city's social life. The cost of the building and furnishings was $46,000. Kerosene lamps gave way to gas jets in 1877, followed by incandescent lamps in 1887. The three-story brick building had fifty rooms in addition to the office, dining room, and parlors. The Joplin Hotel was torn down in 1906 and the Connor Hotel built on its site. Courtesy of the Joplin Historical Society

Interior of the Joplin Hotel lobby around 1900. From the postcard collection of Ron Mosbaugh

Charles Schifferdecker lived in this house when he opened Schifferdecker Gardens on the grounds in 1876. The basic structure has been remodeled by Mr. and Mrs. Elwood McCune, but much of the house and grounds remain the same as they were in Schifferdecker's time. The depressions which once were bowling lanes in the meadow can still be seen as can the many springs and the cave where Schifferdecker cooled the beer he brewed. Photograph by Charles Snow

Charles Schifferdecker was born at Baden, Germany, in 1851 and emigrated to America in 1869. He came to Joplin in 1875 as a representative of Lemp and Anheuser-Busch breweries and built this house on the northwest corner of Fifth and Sergeant about 1890. Said to be modeled on a German castle, the red-brick structure features an unusual, bas-relief trim, stained-glass windows, a turret, and a pond with a bronze fountain. The house is still standing and is identified with a marker on the Joplin Historical Trail. From the State Historical Society of Missouri

This picture, taken in front of the Schifferdecker residence at Fifth and Sergeant, shows the Schifferdecker family ready for an outing in a tally-ho in the 1890s. From the Dorothea B. Hoover Historical Museum

August C. Michaelis, architect and superintendent of building construction at Joplin for many years, was largely responsible for Joplin's appearance. Trained as a carpenter and builder, he taught himself architecture. His work was described as having the distinguishing characteristics of utility and dignity. His designs included the 1896 Joplin High School, St. John's Hospital, the Congregational and Presbyterian churches as well as the houses of many Joplin residents such as Patrick Murphy, whose Carthage cut-stone home cost $25,000. The Michaelis residence, shown here, is still standing on the east side of the 500 block of Wall. Other examples of his work still in existence include J. A. Hewitt's residence at 314 Sergeant, E. J. Overley's house at the southwest corner of Eleventh and Connor, and The Model in the 400 block of Main. From the Dorothea B. Hoover Historical Museum

St. John's Hospital.

A. C. Michaelis residence.

E. J. Overley residence.

J. A. Hewitt residence.

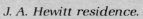

The Model.

3
Chapter

The Mines and the Miners

by Bob Phillips

(Based on the KODE-TV series written and narrated by Bob Phillips)

It was called the Tri-State District. It was roughly thirty-five miles in diameter, covering part of southwest Missouri, northeast Oklahoma, and southeast Kansas, and it was the richest lead and zinc mining area in the civilized world. It produced many millionaires, untold wealth in commerce and industry, and was recognized around the globe.

In Missouri, it stretched north to Alba and Neck City, east to Carthage; in the west, it reached Galena and Baxter Springs, Kansas; to the south, Miami and Picher, Oklahoma, were the boundaries. From this vast field, only the mines of the Picher area are considered worth mining today. The glory days of the others have passed into history.

The two minerals which spawned the Tri-State District were left in the ground somewhere between 400 and 600 million years ago. The warm waters of the Cordilleran Sea, stretching from the Rockies to the Ozark Mountains, dissolved the sedimentary rocks with their impurities and deposited them in the crevices and pockets formed by the upheaval of the Springfield Plateau. The Plateau slopes from east to west, leveling off in the Tri-State District where the minerals were most heavily deposited.

Lead. . . .a common enough substance, really. One of the oldest metals used by man, it's easy to recognize with its peculiar cube shapes and the way it glitters in the light. In its own way, it is as valuable as gold. No home in the world is furnished without lead in some form. . . .It is in the paint, glass, materials for construction, insulation, solder. It is mined in two forms, galena (lead sufide) or carbonate of lead, commonly called "dry bone."

Zinc is mined as sphalerite (sulfide of zinc). Distinguished mostly by its color, it is called by many names: jack, rosin jack, or black jack. In the Tri-State District, it was first thrown out as useless rubble. Today it is used for roofing, engraving plates, batteries, water tanks, telegraph wires, paint bases, and metal coatings. It has a low melting point, molds easily, can be cleaned without injury, and lasts practically forever.

Lead and zinc are often found together, sometimes at grass roots level, other times in large chambers along subterranean waterways at depths of from 60 to 300 feet.

The first miners simply dug a shaft by hand, stopping now and then to drill a hole and dynamite a likely spot. The ore was loaded in a tub or bucket and hoisted to the surface by windlass, operated by human or animal power. The ore was cleaned by sluicing with water or separated in a jig, a box with a screen bottom which was agitated in a tank of water. The cleaned ore was then taken to a smelter where it was melted and cleaned of impurities, formed into pigs of lead, and shipped to the steel mills in the east.

The Miner was sculpted by Puccini Stefano in Italian marble in 1966. Ray Sharp of Joplin was the model for the statue commissioned by George A. Spiva in memory of his father, George N. Spiva. It stood by the fountain in the Spiva Park at the northeast corner of Fourth and Main until recent accidental damage forced its removal. Photograph by Charles Snow

47

But as the lead which could be reached by these shallow, hand-dug shafts ran out, the deep mines came into being.

What must it have been like to work in the mines? Today, the few lead and zinc mines still operating in the Tri-State District are closed to the casual observer. But the Van Hoff mine, near Picher, Oklahoma, allows visitors below to see what was once a producing mine. Worked extensively after the First World War, it retains to this day the fascination that these massive, man-made caverns exerted on every miner.

Today, veteran miners still go down the 178-foot shaft in a bucket hung precariously from a single steel cable, the only conveyance to the strange world below. In the place of the early miners' "sunshine lamps," which burned oil, they now wear battery or carbide lamps. Where once a horse lowered the bucket, a machine now does the job. As the bucket drops through a wooden-beamed shaft only five feet wide, sunlight vanishes and water drips from the walls. At 178 feet, the temperature is a comfortable sixty-five degrees, but the humidity quickly becomes oppressive.

Leaving the bucket, the miner enters a shaft which reaches a quarter of a mile in all directions. Here is almost indescribable beauty . . .grottoes never touched by sunlight, flowing underground streams, rivers of crystal clarity and biting temperatures where eyeless fish have evolved.

The heading, or present upper level of operations, is the scene of activity as miners prepare to drill holes in the bedrock with steam drills. The holes will be filled with dynamite which, it is hoped, will open new veins of lead and zinc ore when detonated. After the explosion, the miners will load the ore buckets, a back-breaking job. Miners can remember filling 100 buckets each day for a salary of a nickel a bucket.

When the bucket is loaded, it must be towed to the lifting point on a narrow gauge track. . . .by a mule. Stubborn, contrary, and at best an individualist, the mule wrote a large chapter in the mining story. He readily adapted to the rigorous life underground. In fact, many were born in the mines and never left them. Miners tell of mules, brought above ground for the first time, who went mad when they saw sunlight.

The water problem constantly plagues miners. In the early days, many shafts were abandoned because of seepage from underground streams. With the development of steam and gasoline powered pumps, this problem was minimized and a large number of the closed mines were re-opened.

Miners were, as a group, hard-working, optimistic believers in luck: the big strike was just a few feet farther down, to the east, on a line with the North Star, somewhere. The names they gave their

This 400-pound specimen of lead and zinc blende shows the distinctive cubical formation which helped the miner identify the mineral. This is one of the many outstanding specimens on display at the Tri-State Mineral Museum in Schifferdecker Park. *From* The Mines and the Miners; *courtesy of Bob Phillips*

Simply titled "A New Mine," this early postcard shows a typical mine in the Joplin area. *From the postcard collection of Ron Mosbaugh*

mines were as colorful as they were: Yellow Dog, Grasshopper, Windy Bill, Uno, Ino, Damfino, Quick Seven, Swindle Deep, Golden Rod, Providence, Morning Star, and the Ten O'Clock. And a remarkable number of the miners actually did make, if not a fortune, at least a comfortable amount.

Once the ore was dug from the ground, it was crushed and milled. It was during this process that zinc was separated from lead, and for some time in the Tri-State District, thrown away. The ore was then smelted and run into pigs of lead.

One of the most interesting developments in the smelting of lead was the process invented by E. O. Bartlett. First used at the smelter owned by Moffet and Sergeant, this process used flannel bags, eighteen inches in diameter and thirty-three feet long, which were attached to the pipes which drew the fumes from the flue during the smelting process. A condensation process resulted in pure white lead, one of the components of fine paint for many years.

Today, it is economically unfeasible to operate a lead or zinc mine unless 7% or more of the ore is pure. In most shafts in the Tri-State District, the percentage has fallen to 4½% or 5%.

But the demand for lead and zinc is again beginning to rise. In the United States, lead is used mainly today for electric storage batteries. Twice as much lead is used for this as for any other purpose. Its next most important use is in making tetraethyl lead for gasoline.

Lead absorbs sound vibrations and, because of new federal rules setting maximum noise levels, is being used extensively in new buildings. Factory machinery is often set on lead mats because lead also absorbs vibrations. And of course it is one of the best shielding materials against x-rays or radiation.

Piles of chat and waste are, for the most part, all that remain of what was once the greatest lead and zinc mining district in the world. People of the Tri-State area pass these remnants every day, but there are few who pause to reflect on their significance. This battered, gouged, and ruptured earth may not look like much now—indeed, it is perhaps not even worth much, but in its days of sunshine, it brought forth unlimited prosperity, national prominence, and a great sense of local pride. It produced men who began with nothing and ended up millionaires. It produced men with shattered dreams and bitter memories. From this area of dust and rock, dampness and despair, rags and riches, back-breaking work in blinding sun and subterranean darkness, this earth brought forth a singularly admirable breed of men—the miners.

The simplest method of bringing buckets of ore up from the mine shafts was with a man-powered hoist like the one in this photograph. It was also the hardest method. From The Mines and the Miners; *courtesy of Bob Phillips*

As soon as a man could afford a horse, he could move up to a horse-powered hoist, or "horse heister," such as the one shown in this photograph. The horse walked around in a circle, drawing the buckets of ore up from the mine shaft. From The Mines and the Miners; *courtesy of Bob Phillips*

This mining scene shows a typical, two-man mining operation with a horse heister to operate the bucket. *From the Dorothea B. Hoover Historical Museum*

This photograph shows the area where Range Line, a four-lane highway lined with motels, restaurants, and other business establishments, now runs. Notice how many mines were crowded into the small area. *From* The Mines and the Miners; *courtesy of Bob Phillips*

After the ore was mined, it was crushed and separated in a jig, an open box with a screen at the bottom. The top photograph shows an early hand jig, while the bottom one shows a steam-powered jig. *Courtesy of Rolla Stephens*

This collection of mining lamps is on display at the Tri-State Mineral Museum in Schifferdecker Park. From the Tri-State Mineral Museum.

This steam-powered drill was used to drill holes into the hard-rock formations. A charge of dynamite was set off in the holes, blasting loose the ore. One miner sits on a box from the Aetna Powder Company, which provided much of the blasting powder. From The Mines and the Miners; *courtesy of Bob Phillips*

Even in the 1940s, when this aerial photograph was taken, Joplin was surrounded by piles of chat brought up in the mining operations. From the Tri-State Mineral Museum.

This photograph, labeled "Modern Ore Mill," was probably taken in the early 1900s. From the Tri-State Mineral Museum

MODERN ORE MILL. JOPLIN, MO.

This spot beneath the Broadway Bridge is the site of one of the earliest mine shafts sunk in what came to be known as the Joplin Mining Camp. Marked here with a pick, shovel, and miner's lunch bucket for Joplin's Centennial celebration, it is rarely noticed by the people of Joplin as they hurry by today. Photograph by Charles Snow

As the mines have been abandoned, nature has slowly recaptured the area. The building foundation is all that remains of this once-active mine. From The Mines and the Miners; *courtesy of Bob Phillips*

4
Chapter

The Building Years

1898–1917

store in 1890. In 1902 the store moved to Fifth and Main and a three-story building which was torn down in 1917 to make room for the present five-story building. Albert Newman and Gabe Newburger started Newman's at 517 Main in 1898 and in 1910 built a five-story building at the southwest corner of Sixth and Main. Albert and Robert Ramsay opened the Ramsay Department Store in 1910 as part of a chain that included stores at Carthage, Iola, Pittsburg, and Atchison, Kansas.

In 1910 Joplin was the only city in Jasper County that was "wet," a condition which meant that people from Oklahoma and Kansas as well as other counties in Missouri visited Joplin to buy liquor. As a center for bootlegging activities, Joplin retained its image as a wild city despite the fact that ordinary citizens were usually not involved in the illegal traffic.

The early 1900s were years of optimism for most Americans, including those who lived in Joplin. Despite the Panic of 1907, which resulted in the closing of many mines as the price of ore dropped, the people of Joplin took life in stride and enjoyed the pleasures of the time. In 1910 the Miners baseball team from Joplin won the championship of the Western Association. Fight promotions and wrestling programs drew big crowds. Schifferdecker Electric Park with its beautiful electric light displays and carnival rides competed for popularity with Lakeside Park with its gardens and boating attractions. Both could be easily reached by the electric streetcar line which now connected Carthage, Webb City, Carterville, and Joplin.

Progress was the key word in Joplin. In April 1911, just 7½ years after Kitty Hawk, a test flight was made of an aluminum airplane built in a shop on Wall. According to the newspaper account, the plane "ascended into the air and maintained a fair rate of speed."

Better roads and the advent of Henry Ford's Model T brought new business, new people, and new excitement to Joplin. In 1914 Joplin became a second-class city and the first city in Missouri to operate under the commission form of government. It would have been difficult to find anyone in that progressive, optimistic town to predict the changes which would come from the guns that were beginning to rumble in Europe.

Clubs have played an important part in Joplin's history. This photograph of the Bachelor's Club in 1898 indicates that bachelorhood may not have been a desired state, however: try to find a smiling face in the group. Courtesy of the Joplin Historical Society

Farming operations in the Joplin area became mechanized in the early 1900s. This photograph shows a steam-powered threshing machine. From the Dorothea B. Hoover Historical Museum

This late 1890s photograph shows the interesting structure called the Columbian Block, located at 418 Main. Its twin cupolas—removed by later renovations—are visible in many photographs around the turn of the century. Notice the store to the right, which advertises "High Class Millinery and Ladies Out-fitting." From the Dorothea B. Hoover Historical Museum

In 1876 Joplin formed a Jockey Club and Fair Association. A race track was built on a tract of land bounded now by Twentieth, Seventeenth, Murphy Avenue, and Maiden Lane. Later known as Barbee Park, the race track remained in use well into the 1900s. In this picture, circa 1890, the trotters are rounding the curve of the track. From the State Historical Society of Missouri

Percy Wenrich, "The Joplin Kid," was born in 1880 in Joplin. He attended public schools and studied organ and piano with his mother prior to attending Chicago Musical College. Already an accomplished musician while still in his teens, Wenrich is known to have slipped into the House of Lords to hear such famous ragtime and blues musicians as Scott Joplin and Blind Boone. Wenrich entered vaudeville with his wife, Dolly Connolly, and toured the vaudeville circuits for fifteen years. His works include the operetta Castles in the Air and the musical comedy The Right Girl. He is best known for his many popular songs, including Put On Your Old Grey Bonnet, Moonlight Bay, When You Wore a Tulip and I Wore a Big Red Rose, Sweet Cider Time, Baby, Silver Bell, and Sail Along Silvery Moon. Wenrich died in 1952 and is buried in Fairview Cemetery in Joplin. Photograph by Latour; from the Dorothea B. Hoover Historical Museum

The Young Men's Christian Association (YMCA) was an active organization with its offices on Fourth Street between Main and Virginia. In this 1902 photograph, the office of the Daily Globe can also be seen. In 1918, the Globe purchased the YMCA building and physically joined the two. The building has been remodeled several times and is still the home of the Joplin Globe. From the State Historical Society of Missouri

As were many other libraries throughout the United States, the Joplin Free Library was built through a gift from Andrew Carnegie. Built in 1902 on the northwest corner of Ninth and Wall, the library has been placed on the National Register of Historic Places. A new library opened in 1980 on the site of the old Connor Hotel. From the postcard collection of Ron Mosbaugh

The Junge Baking Company plant at Eighteenth and Joplin in 1903. Established by Albert Junge, it was the first major bakery in Joplin. Courtesy of Alberta Junge York

This young saleswoman for the Junge Baking Company is surrounded by products familiar to Joplinites in the early 1900s—Quaker-etts, Butter Thin Wafers, Pok-A-Dot Biscuits, Banquet Wafers, Junge Baking Company Sodas, and Junge Pound Cakes. From Alberta Junge York

Considerable time and effort must have gone into the preparation of this Junge Baking Company Float for one of Joplin's patriotic parades. Courtesy of Alberta Junge York

These workers at the Junge Baking Company, circa 1906, packed Quaker Crackers in handmade wooden boxes. Another Junge product was Pok-A-Dot Crackers. In making the crackers, the dough was folded several times and then stamped out to size; at the same time the cracker was "pinned" in several places by docker pins to prevent it from swelling out of shape while in the oven. The distinctive pattern left by the docker pins was the inspiration for the crackers' name. From Alberta Junge York

Change the Rhythm of the Times

1917–1941

When the United States declared war on Germany on April 6, 1917, the prospects for an Allied victory looked bleak. Germany was in control of the sea lanes, the French army was in a state of mutiny, Britain's resources were almost exhausted, and the U.S. had only 200,000 men in the army. Yet most Joplinites, like most Americans, were convinced that we could win the war and make the world safe for democracy.

Nationalistic feeling ran high and Joplinites were inclined to forget the many contributions of the German community. The Germania Hall, center of many social activities in the past, was closed and deeded to the Red Cross. A group of rowdies threw rocks through the windows of the German Insurance Company, located in the Miners' Bank Building, simply because it had the word "German" in its name.

After the Selective Service Act was passed on May 18, Jim Leonard was named head of the Joplin draft board. Some 3,700 men from Joplin went into the military service.

The corner of Fourth and Main, where the First National Bank is now located, was known as Liberty Lot. Bond rallies were held with speakers giving four-minute speeches. Departing servicemen listened to the speeches, ate complimentary dinners at the House of Lords, and marched to the railway accompanied by a band.

When news of the signing of the armistice was received on the morning of November 11, 1918, revelers began to appear on the street almost immediately. Before the day was over thousands of people thronged the city and paraded through the streets. Although eighty-three Joplinites had lost their lives, the war to end all wars was over.

The population of Joplin had grown to nearly 36,000. But suddenly, the newly opened mining fields in Oklahoma began to draw miners and their families away. Despite the shuttle trains, the buddy cars, and the best efforts of local businessmen, the miners moved away. By 1920 Joplin's population had dropped to 29,902.

Joplin was changing rapidly. It had to change if it was going to survive. By 1926 Joplin had begun a concentrated effort to draw new industry and tourists to the area. Its park system was the envy of many larger cities, and its social events, such as the annual Easter egg hunt sponsored by the Lions Club, drew thousands of spectators.

But all the parties and parks couldn't hide the fact that times were getting harder. People were worried; events seemed to be going out of control, changing too fast. In 1929 a city lamp cleaner committed suicide, apparently despondent over the changes occurring when the city lighting system was sold to the Empire District Electric Company. Change . . . it was the rhythm of the times.

Today, the Great Depression evokes images of distraught speculators committing suicide; gray, exhausted people standing in

Fourth Street looking west with the Connor Hotel on the right, circa 1920. In the background can be seen the Miners' Bank Building. From the postcard collection of Ron Mosbaugh

99

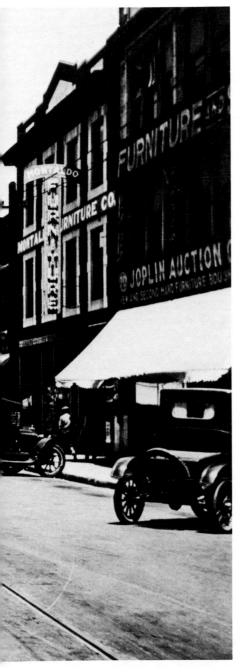

soup lines; and the formerly rich selling apples on streetcorners. But for most people in Joplin the reality of the depression was a relentless increase in the everyday problems of finding work, making do, getting by. Few had the time or inclination to worry about the social impact of this new economic crisis.

For that matter, there were encouraging signs such as the 1930 census which showed Joplin's population at 33,454, an increase of eleven percent over 1920. Forty-three mines were still in operation, plans were underway for the building of the Joplin Stockyards, the opening of the Mineral Museum was held in 1931, and the Chamber of Commerce was working to bring new industry to Joplin. People weren't prepared for the closing of the Eagle-Picher smelter and the resulting unemployment.

But one industry was thriving—bootlegging. Although it would be 1933 before Prohibition was legally ended, in Joplin it was possible to buy all the liquor you wanted. And with the illegal sale of liquor came the attendant criminal element, re-creating the "sin city" reputation Joplin had known at the turn of the century.

Will Rogers visited Joplin in 1933. "I went to school at Neosho," he said. "They used to say Carthage was the prettiest town, Neosho had the prettiest girls, and Joplin was supposed to be the toughest joint in this part of the country. Our parents used to scare us with Joplin just like they would scare us with the Devil."

In the 1930s, Joplin was a cooling-off place for criminals from all over the United States. There seems to have been a tacit agreement that as long as they behaved themselves within the city limits, their other crimes would be ignored. Until April 14, 1933.

On that date, Joplin police received a tip that someone living in a small house on Thirty-fourth and Oak Ridge Drive was involved in a Neosho robbery. When the police arrived with a search warrant, gunfire broke out, leaving Policeman Wes Harryman and Detective

This photograph of Joplin's Main Street was taken looking north from Eighth around 1919. The Clarketon Hotel is in the left foreground. The Joplin Furniture Store, shown on the left, is still standing and in business. Notice the tracks and overhead wires for the electric streetcars. From the Joplin Chamber of Commerce

101

This army recruiting effort took place during World War I. According to the sign, the German machine gun was captured by the 27th Division. Many recruiting efforts and bond sales were held at the corner of Fourth and Main, which was called Liberty Lot. From the Dorothea B. Hoover Historical Museum

The Joplin City Hall on the southeast corner of Second and Joplin, circa 1920. From the postcard collection of Ron Mosbaugh

The nursing class which graduated in 1919 from St. John's School of Nursing had already seen the devastating effects of disease when an influenza epidemic hit Joplin during the winter of 1917-18. From St. John's Medical Center

Harry McGuinnis dead. The gunmen got away, but they were identified: Clyde Barrow, Ivy (Buck) Barrow, Bonnie Parker, and Blanche Barrow. Pictures on the front page of the *Joplin Globe* of Bonnie and Clyde with the dead bodies of the policemen signaled an end to the easy life for criminals in Joplin.

President Roosevelt's New Deal affected Joplin as the various programs for civil works led to the enlargement of the federal courthouse and post office building, the replacement of brick sidewalks with concrete, the installation of storm sewers, and the filling of old mine shafts and caves.

And life went on. Tryouts for a leading role in the Paramount movie, *Island of Souls*, were held in Joplin, with Marjorie Hunt taking first place, followed by Helen Marrs and Sara James. Movies such as *King Kong* played to a full house.

In 1937 the Joplin Junior College was established in the newly renovated building which had served as the high school from 1896 to 1918 at the corner of Fourth and Byers.

In 1939 the Joplin Little Theatre presented its first play, *Three Cornered Moon*. Joplinites could relax and enjoy themselves with the minimum wage now established at forty cents an hour, the beginning of a forty-hour work week, and the new Social Security Act which promised help for the elderly, disabled, and dependent children. Even though times were changing, surely happy days were almost here again.

For years, people in Joplin met at the corner of Fourth and Main where the elaborate face was cut into the decoration of the Keystone Hotel. The building is no longer standing. From the Dorothea B. Hoover Historical Museum

Central School on Eighth between Joplin and Wall served as Joplin's secondary school for many years. This photograph was taken November 11, 1919. Memorial Hall now occupies this spot. From the Dorothea B. Hoover Historical Museum

The Scottish Rite Cathedral of Free Masonry is located on the southeast corner of Fifth and Byers. It was built in 1919 and has been in continuous use since that time. From the Joplin Printing Company

The New Joplin Theatre, shown here around 1920, was located at the southwest corner of Seventh and Joplin. Also called the Schubert Theatre, it was razed in the 1930s. From the postcard collection of Ron Mosbaugh

The annual Lions Club Easter egg hunt in Schifferdecker Park drew huge crowds in the 1920s. From the Joplin Chamber of Commerce

Cunningham Park at Twenty-sixth and Maiden Lane was known for its beautiful flower gardens. Today the park has a swimming pool, and the shelter house is used for group picnics, weddings, and family reunions throughout the mild weather. From the postcard collection of Ron Mosbaugh

This aerial view shows Junge Park, just south of the Junge Baking Company building at 1810 South Main. Albert Junge's green thumb created this delightful garden, complete with flowers raised in the Junge's own greenhouse and a miniature railroad. Courtesy of Alberta Junge York

A good description of the animated diorama at Junge Park was published in the March-April 1941 issue of The Round Table: "Visitors to Joplin, Missouri, and the townspeople as well, proclaim Junge's three-dimensional billboard one of the finest outdoor presentations in the country. In reality, it is a colorful diorama with animated lighting effects portraying events appropriate to the season or occasion. Great care is expended in these seasonal dramatizations which attract wide interest at all times of the year. This animated colorama is further enhanced by the beautiful garden setting on the grounds of the Junge Baking Company. The garden is large and contains a myriad of brightly colored flowers, smooth green lawn, and a well-formed background of shrubbery and trees. The park-like appearance created is indeed a tribute to the management, employees, and the community as a whole." From Alberta Junge York

A nighttime view of the autumn scene of the Junge's diorama: as the figures moved across the scene, the music of "Indian Love Call" played. From Alberta Junge York

Crystal Cave was discovered in 1893 by miners working for Henry Weymann. Weymann immediately bought the mining rights for the area between Third, Fourth, Gray, and Melvin. The cave was lined with magnificent calcite crystals, the largest known in any country. Weymann hoped to preserve it in its original state for future generations of geologists and mineralogists. Unfortunately, the water problem common to so many mines flooded Crystal Cave, and it is now closed. A marker indicates its location on the Joplin Historical Trail. From the postcard collection of Ron Mosbaugh

Crystal Cave was used as a meeting place by various clubs during the summer months of the 1920s before the advent of air conditioning. The calcite crystals glittered and reflected light, making it a spot of storybook beauty. From the Dorothea B. Hoover Historical Museum

Schifferdecker Park, consisting of sixty acres, was a gift to the city from Charles Schifferdecker. In the 1920s it had flower gardens, a zoo, a dance pavilion, camping sites, and a free movie pavilion. From the State Historical Society of Missouri

This scene was taken at the Schifferdecker Municipal Golf Course during the 1925 Missouri Open Tournament playoff match between Eddie Held and Edw. B. Dudley, Jr. From the Joplin Chamber of Commerce

The Schifferdecker Golf Course was a popular spot for sports enthusiasts in the 1920s when such pros as Horton Smith were playing in Joplin. From the Joplin Chamber of Commerce

Witmer Park, now called Wildcat Park, is located in south Joplin just within the city limits. Silver Creek and Shoal Creek meet at this point, and the cool waters have proved inviting to swimmers and boaters for many years. From the Joplin Chamber of Commerce

McClelland Park, located just south of Joplin on Shoal Creek, has retained much of the wilderness beauty seen in this page from a 1920s publication of the chamber of commerce. From the Joplin Chamber of Commerce

CUNNINGHAM PARK

1. Picnic Tables, Band Stand and winding walks.

2. Cunningham Park is noted for its beautiful Flower Gardens.

3. Swimming Pool.

Three scenes of Cunningham Park at Twenty-Sixth and Maiden Lane from a promotional brochure published by the chamber of commerce in the 1920s. From the Joplin Chamber of Commerce

The intersection of Fifth and Sergeant looking north in the 1920s. Charles Schifferdecker's house is on the left, Ed Zelleken's house is visible in the left background, and W. H. Picher's house is on the right. All three residences are still standing. From the Dorothea B. Hoover Historical Museum

The Joplin General Osteopathic Hospital was opened in August 1937 at the northeast corner of Fourth and Moffet. The hospital moved to its new location at 932 East Thirty-fourth in September 1963 and was named Oak Hill Osteopathic Hospital. The brick addition shown to the right in this picture is still standing and is used for the Mo-Kan Boy Scout Headquarters. Courtesy of Oak Hill Osteopathic Hospital

In 1931 Joe H. Myers, a member of the City Park Board, started the Tri-State Mineral Museum in an old concession structure at Schifferdecker Park. The purpose of the museum was to display both the mineral resources of the district and the finished products of lead and zinc, and to depict the mining industry by means of miniatures. The miniatures were designed and built by Sam Madden, a park board carpenter, and Myers. Harry G. Packer gave the initial private collection and became the museum's first custodian. The Tri-State Mineral Museum draws thousands of visitors from all over the world every year to see the unique collection of rare and irreplaceable specimens from the lead and zinc mines of the area. Photograph by Head of Joplin; from the State Historical Society of Missouri

Established in 1902, the Joplin Transfer and Storage Company was active in handling and transporting heavy mining equipment used in the district. The firm is now the Joplin Mayflower agency and is located at 507 East Fifth. This photograph circa 1936. From Joplin Transfer and Storage Company

Matt and Kit Vickery, well-known Joplin mining history buffs, helped acquire many of the mineral samples and old mining tools which are now on display at the Tri-State Mineral Museum. Matt Vickery is shown in this 1930s view. Photograph by Head of Joplin; from the State Historical Society of Missouri

Joplin's Main Street in the 1930s. The photograph was taken looking north from the mid-700 block. The traffic light is at the intersection of U. S. Highway 66 and Missouri Highway 43. From the Dorothea B. Hoover Historical Museum

The Unity Baptist Church was formed in 1901 when the Second Baptist and St. John Baptist churches combined. The church was located at Seventh and Kentucky until a storm demolished the building. Worship services were held in the Jasper County Courthouse until a new edifice was built at 511 East Seventh in 1904 as a gift of Tom Connor. In 1939 the church moved to its present location at 615 Minnesota, shown here. From the Unity Baptist Church

Flying has fascinated Joplinites since the 1911 test flight of the aluminum plane made in Joplin. Harrison Harper, second from left in the upper photograph, learned to fly in 1928 in a World War I vintage OX5 JN-4, commonly called a Jenny. In 1933 Harper operated the old Joplin Municipal Airport, which was located on the same spot as the present airport. A WPA project in 1935-37 constructed three runways for the Joplin airport. After serving in World War II, Harper constructed the Harper Airport on west Seventh, and he operated it from 1948 to 1953. From the postcard collection of Ron Mosbaugh

HARPER AIRCRAFT COMPANY
MUNICIPAL AIRPORT
JOPLIN, MO.

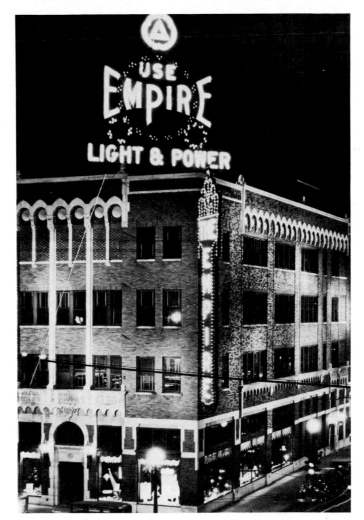

The Empire District Electric Company's offices at 602 Joplin were a good advertisement for electric lights in this pre-energy crisis picture. From the Joplin Printing Company

Grand Falls, a natural fall on Shoal Creek south of Joplin, was used to generate electricity for Joplin for many years and has been a favorite recreational spot with Joplinites. From the Dorothea B. Hoover Historical Museum

There were prizes for the lucky people whose names were drawn from the huge barrel set up during Fiesta Days in downtown Joplin in the 1930s and 1940s. Notice the hats with fringe on them—a tradition for Fiesta Days. Photograph by Baird Studios

The Joplin Fiesta Parade in 1940 heads north on Main Street. Like many other activities, the Fiesta ended during the war years. Photograph by Baird Studios

Joplin's Fiesta Queen for 1940 was Billye Grattis. Courtesy of Helen Knight Chickering

If you look closely, you can see the diver climbing the pole, at left just above the sporting goods sign, for his leap into the tank below. The crowd at this Fiesta in the early 1940s is typical of the numbers that thronged the city for the annual festival. Photograph by Baird Studios

6
Chapter

Fear and Hope

1941–1970

An aerial view of Joplin taken in 1955. From the State Historical Society of Missouri

Mr. and Mrs. John W. Freeman started Freeman Hospital with a gift of their house. Located at Twentieth and Sergeant, the 1911 structure was bequeathed to the city in memory of Orly Freeman, their son, in 1922. The building in this picture is presently an office building since the 1975 completion of the multi-million dollar Freeman Hospital at its new location, 1102 West Thirty-second. Courtesy of Joplin Chamber of Commerce

This photograph of downtown Joplin was taken from the Spiva Park on the northeast corner of Fourth and Main. The Keystone Hotel on the left and the Connor Hotel on the right have been demolished. From the Joplin Chamber of Commerce

The Forest Park Baptist Church was one of the first in the Joplin area. This photo shows the current church building at Seventh and Highview. Courtesy of the Joplin Printing Company

When the first United Methodist Church on the northwest corner of Fourth and Byers was struck by lightning in 1963, the steeple had to be removed. Courtesy of the First United Methodist Church

James Langston Hughes was born in 1902 in Joplin. Hughes received a Guggenheim Fellowship in 1935, the Rosenwald Fellowship in 1941, an honorary Doctor of Literature from Lincoln University of Pennsylvania in 1943, and the NAACP Spingarn Medal in 1960. He was elected a member of the select National Institute of Arts and Letters in 1961. According to Donald Dickerson, director of Readers' Service at University Library, Hughes is "probably the most widely read American Negro writer of the twentieth century." A poet, author, and playwright, Hughes wrote Not Without Laughter, The Ways of the White Folks, The Big Sea, Shakespeare in Harlem, and the series, Semple Speaks His Mind, Semple Takes a Wife, and Semple Stakes a Claim. The New York Times said that Hughes' works were "stripped, laconic, set to an unheard blues beat." Shortly after his death in 1967, a portion of Broadway including the viaduct was renamed Langston Hughes Boulevard in his honor. From the Dorothea B. Hoover Historical Museum

This group of junior high boys prepared their own version of the German Turnverein Band for Joplin's eighty-eighth birthday party in 1961. Courtesy of Mrs. Gale Graham

Missouri Governor Warren E. Hearnes is shown here in 1965 presenting Colonel Clark E. Anglen with the commission for the Missouri Governor's Mounted Guard. It was the first mounted guard commissioned in the nation; several other states have since organized a mounted guard. Governor Hearnes was in Joplin to dedicate the Missouri Southern State College campus at the same time. Courtesy of Helen Knight Chickering

ald Eagle, a stainless steel sculpture
Nancy Kissel Clark, Joplin native
culptor, was lent to the city of
oplin for its first Fall Festival of the
rts in 1967. The event was staged by
the Joplin Council for the Arts and
produced by Mary Curtis Warten.
Following the festival the Joplin
Council for the Arts, through private
contributions, purchased the sculpture for permanent installation in the
Joplin Municipal Building. Courtesy
of Mary Curtis Warten.

New York Times *art critic John Canaday, Thomas Hart Benton, and Mary Curtis Warten (left to right) are shown at the opening of the Thomas Hart Benton Retrospective Exhibition on March 23, 1973. The exhibition was held at the Spiva Art Center on the Missouri Southern State College campus. From Mary Curtis Warten*

This photograph of the interior of the Joplin Municipal Building shows the sculpture, Bald Eagle, by Nancy Kissel Clark, on the left. Above the doors is the Thomas Hart Benton Mural, Joplin at the Turn of the Century, 1896-1906. *Courtesy of Mary Curtis Warten*

Bob Cummings, award-winning actor and director, veteran of more than 100 movies and four television series, has had a career spanning forty-eight years. Charles Clarence Robert Orville Cummings was born June 9, 1910, in Joplin. Orville Wright, a friend of his doctor father, was his godfather and an influence on Cummings' love of aviation. He soloed in 1927 at Joplin in the No. 1 Travelair Biplane. In 1937 Cummings received the first flight instructor's rating ever issued. He has flown over fifty years without an accident. He began his studies in aeronautical engineering at the Carnegie Institute of Technology, but the Depression forced him to drop out. He received a scholarship to the American Academy of Dramatic Arts in New York and began his career. Realizing that there was a demand for English actors, he borrowed on an insurance policy, went to England for a month, and returned as "Blade Stanhope Conway," making his debut in The Roof in 1931. When the British craze ended, he went to Hollywood and changed his name back to Bob Cummings. His movie credits include King's Row, Dial M for Murder, The Petty Girl, The Carpetbaggers, Stagecoach, For Heaven's Sake, and How to Be Very, Very Popular. Cummings has appeared in many television shows including his own series, The Bob Cummings Show, which he also directed. Several episodes for this show were filmed in Joplin. He received an Emmy award for best actor in 1955 for his dramatic role in Twelve Angry Men. Interested in organic foods and natural vitamins, he is the author of Stay Young and Vital. Cummings is married to Regina Maria Young and has two children, Michele and Charles Clarence III. He has five other children by a former marriage. Courtesy of Bob Cummings

As part of Joplin's first annual Fall Festival of the Arts in October 1967, Bob Cummings was welcomed back to Joplin for the celebration of "Bob Cummings Day." From the Joplin Printing Company

The aerial view of the Missouri Southern State College campus shows the Fred Hughes Stadium in the foreground. The college, located at Newman and Duquesne in the northeast section of Joplin, graduated 560 students in 1978, more than twice the number in the college's first graduating class in 1969. Courtesy of Missouri Southern State College

Robert Higgs was born in Anderson, Missouri, on August 14, 1916, and began painting in oils and watercolors while he was young. He studied at the Kansas City Art Institute and the Academy of Fine Arts in Chicago. Higgs came to Joplin in 1939 to work for the Joplin Printing Company as art director. One of the charter members of the Ozark Artists' Guild and first president of the group, he produced more than 3,500 works before his death in 1967. His work has been exhibited in New Mexico, Oklahoma, Kansas, Missouri, Texas, Ohio, and California. He was a member associate of the American Watercolor Society and received a purchase award in 1965. His paintings are included in the collections of the Ford Motor Company, IBM Corporation, Martha's Vineyard Art Association, the Spiva Art Center, and many others. A memorial exhibit of Higgs' work was featured when the Spiva Art Center on the Missouri Southern State College campus opened in 1967. Courtesy of Mrs. Marie Higgs Murray

Sibley Barn by Robert Higgs. Higgs worked in many mediums, including watercolor, dry brush prints, oils, and polymers. He was generous with his time in teaching others. Higgs served with the Army during World War II. Some of his paintings were published in Japan and the United States as an accurate chronicle of the war in the Pacific. Courtesy of Mrs. Marie Higgs Murray

The College Union on the Missouri Southern State College Campus. A one million-dollar addition was completed in 1979 and named in honor of Dr. Leon Billingsly, first president of MSSC, who died in 1978. Courtesy of Joplin Chamber of Commerce

The Spiva Art Center was named for George A. Spiva, long a philanthropic supporter of the arts in Joplin, who gave $100,000 toward the construction of the fine arts building on the Missouri Southern State College campus. There are two studios in the building and an upper gallery for exhibiting traveling collections and other fine art works. Courtesy of Missouri Southern State College

The Joplin Municipal Airport, located north of the city, is served by Ozark Air Lines, Frontier Airlines, and Executive Trans Air. In 1978, a record 134,706 airline passengers passed through the boarding and departing gates at the airport. Courtesy of the Joplin Chamber of Commerce

Cozetta Thompson has been a leader in the Black community since the 1960s. She was elected to three terms on the Joplin R-8 Board of Education, was the Seventh District State Human Rights Commissioner to Jefferson City 1976-77, is a former administrator of the Joplin Business College, and currently is an employment counselor with a Joplin firm. From the Memorial High School Talon, 1969

The international headquarters of the Pentecostal Church of God of America are located at Third and Main in this modern building which also houses the Commerce Bank of Joplin. The fourteen-story building in the background is the Messenger Towers housing complex for the elderly, built and operated by the Pentecostal Church of God. Photograph by Jim Mueller; courtesy of the Joplin Chamber of Commerce

The Sperry Vickers plant at 2800 West Tenth employs more than 700 people in the manufacture of hydraulic units, parts, and components. Courtesy of the Joplin Chamber of Commerce

The Joplin Historical Society sponsored annual Historical Homes Tours from 1967 to 1973. This photograph, taken in 1968, shows Suzanne Childress Sharp in her home, the original Henry Weymann residence at 508 Sergeant. Built in 1892, the house features an arched, stained-glass window made of leaded panels of various types of stained glass including opalescent and "jewels." The house had its own water distiller, circulating hot water heating system, speaking tubes in each room connected to the servants' quarters on the third floor, and a central vacuum cleaning unit with outlets in each room. A quaint playhouse in the backyard, built for a niece of Weymanns', was the regular meeting place for the Lambda Alpha Lambda sorority in the early 1900s. Courtesy of the Joplin Historical Society

Pictured during the 1968 Historical Homes Tour sponsored by the Joplin Historical Society is Lavon Lanyon Smoot in her home at 212 North Pearl. Abstracts show that this house, built for Reuben S. Lanyon, was constructed on part of the original grant of John C. Cox. Built in 1890, the house has been changed very little since that date. It is noted for the handsome inlaid floors, paneling, doors, and woodwork, especially the balustrade and stairway. Courtesy of the Joplin Historical Society

7
Chapter

Mining the Future

The 1970s seemed to bring more than their share of trouble to Joplin. As the Vietnam War wound down, Joplin found it had lost twenty-three people in a war that had caused tremendous dissension in the United States.

Nature took a harsh turn in the 1970s. A tornado skipped through the city in 1971; fire destroyed the courthouse in 1972; 7.7 inches of rain fell in twelve hours in 1976, flooding the downtown with three to four feet of water and causing millions of dollars worth of damage on the eve of the city's celebration of the U. S. Bicentennial; bitter cold and snowstorms hit the city in 1977 and 1978.

And in perhaps the most widely known disaster to hit Joplin, the Connor Hotel, while being rigged for demolition, collapsed suddenly in November 1978, killing two men and trapping Albert Summers in a small chamber where he lay helpless for three days while the nation watched the rescue efforts. Miraculously, he suffered only minor injuries.

But good things were happening in Joplin, too. Certainly the most exciting and ambitious project was the Centennial celebration in 1973, and the high point of the celebration was the unveiling of the Thomas Hart Benton mural, *Joplin at the Turn of the Century, 1896-1906.*

Benton was born in Neosho, Missouri, in 1889. During the summer of 1906 he came to the Joplin area to work with a cousin on a surveying party. One Saturday night Benton went to the House of Lords, where he became absorbed in one of the nude paintings that hung above the bar. When the men began to tease Benton, he said he wasn't interested in naked women but was an artist and just wanted to see how the picture was painted. Before the barrage of kidding was over, Benton was challenged to go to the *Joplin American* newspaper and apply for a position as artist on the paper. He got the job, at fourteen dollars a week, and spent the summer drawing cartoons of locally prominent people. Benton went on to become one of the best-known modern American artists.

In May of 1971 a tornado dropped down on the city, causing one death and thousands of dollars worth of damage. This photograph shows the Anderson Trailer Court on Newman Road after the tornado. From Baird Studios

Joplin's Centennial logo was designed by Rita Swanson, Joplin commericial artist. The logo depicts a tree growing out of a miner's hat and symbolizes the city's growth. From the Joplin '73 Centennial Association

T. Frank (Chief) Coulter, 1893-1973. Coulter began his teaching career in Joplin in 1916 as a mathematics teacher at Joplin Senior High School. He loved music and soon became the director of the school's orchestra and, in 1920, the director of the entire music department. During his forty-five year music career, Coulter organized the Senior Girls' Drum and Bugle Corps, Solo and Ensemble Club, Joplin Symphony Orchestra, and the Joplin Music Festival, which was one of the first non-competitive festivals in the country. He was president of the Missouri Music Educators' Association in 1937 and 1949 as well as serving in many other state music organizations. Through his efforts and enthusiasm, the Joplin High School music department grew to be one of the most outstanding in the nation, receiving music honors in nine states. In June of 1972 Coulter was recognized for his accomplishments when he became the fourth person elected to the Missouri Bandmasters' Association Hall of Fame. Courtesy of Connie Coulter Mosbaugh

Leon Kassab, chairman of the Joplin '73 Centennial Commission, and Mayor Lena Beal, Joplin's first woman mayor, are shown on March 23, 1973, at the official opening of the Joplin Centennial celebration. From Mary Curtis Warten

When the Joplin Council for the Arts approached Benton about painting a mural for the town's Centennial celebration, he at first refused. Considered the leading muralist in America, Benton was eighty-two years old and had said that he would not paint any more large-scale paintings after he finished the mural for the Truman Library at Independence, Missouri, in 1961. But the people of Joplin persuaded him to round out his career by returning to the place where it had begun and painting a mural to show how Joplin had looked then. Through the council, Joplin raised $60,000 for the Benton mural, which was placed in the city Municipal Building.

At the time the mural was unveiled, the Joplin Council for the Arts sponsored a Benton retrospective exhibition at the Spiva Art Center on the Missouri Southern State College campus. It was the largest and most diverse exhibition of Benton's work ever held.

As Joplin enters the 1980s, the mining town image has disappeared. Few residents recall the wild times which made Joplin notorious. Most of the mine shafts have been filled in and the piles of chat have been leveled. Yet some of the strength and daring of those early miners lives on in Joplin residents today: a prototype of a battery-operated car of the future is tested on Joplin streets; experiments in the fields of computers, transistors, medicine, and industrial equipment are quietly conducted; new architectural approaches are tried. The town that jack built is using new technology to build the future.

National Guardsmen patrol Main at Thirteenth in the aftermath of the tornado. From Baird Studios

Football is one of the most popular sports in the Joplin area. Parkwood High School won the Class AAAA State High School Championship in 1975 and Memorial High School won the Class AAA Championship in 1976. This picture shows the Missouri Southern State College Lions football team at the Fred Hughes Stadium on the MSSC campus. The Lions were NAIA Division Two champions in 1972. Courtesy of Missouri Southern State College

In 1973 the Joplin '73 Centennial Commission recognized Percy Wenrich's contributions to American music by placing a bronze tablet at his grave in Fairview Cemetery. Inscribed on the tablet is a Wenrich quote: "things that happened at home gave me . . . song titles. The feeling for home . . . gave me the music." Shown in the photograph are Mary Curtis Warten, vice-chairman of the commission, and Leon Kassab, chairman, dressed in turn-of-the-century garb complete with yellow tulip and big red rose of Wenrich's song. Photograph by Charles Snow; from the Joplin '73 Centennial Commission

Joe Beeler was one of the founders of the Cowboy Artists of America. He has twice been honored with the Silver Award for Sculpture of the National Cowboy Hall of Fame and Western Heritage Center as well as the Higgins Ink Award; Meritorious Achievement Award from the Kansas State College of Pittsburg Alumni Association; Colt Award from the Cowboy Artists of America Show; and a Gold Medal for Painting from the Franklin Mint. Beeler designed the Joplin Centennial Medallion for the Centennial celebration. This bronze is entitled Up the Trail. Copyright by the Spiva Art Center, Inc.; reproduced by permission of the Spiva Art Center

Joe Beeler, western artist and sculptor, grew up in Joplin and graduated from Joplin High School in 1949. He attended Joplin Junior College, Tulsa University, Kansas State College at Pittsburg, and the Los Angeles Art Center School. Beeler grew up with a love for Indian and western heritage; his paternal grandmother was a Cherokee Indian, and his father used to dance at powwows. The Spiva Art Center and the Missouri State Council on the Arts presented a Joe Beeler Exhibit from June 20 to July 31, 1973, in conjunction with Joplin's Centennial celebration. With Beeler in this photograph are Joy Spiva Cragin (left) and Suzanne Childress Sharp, who co-chaired the Joe Beeler Exhibit. Courtesy of the Spiva Art Center, Inc.

Dorothea Bliedung Hoover was the daughter of Edmund A. Bliedung, an early Joplinite and partner in the Christman Department Store. (Her brother is the actor John Beal.) Born September 25, 1896, she spent most of her life in Joplin. A graduate of Joplin High School and Wellesley College in Massachusetts, she married David Hoover in 1923, and was active in many facets of community life. She was a co-founder and president of the Joplin Little Theatre; chairman of the Jasper County Women's Division for war bond sales during World War II; member of the Joplin Chamber of Commerce; president of the Jasper County branch of the American Association of University Women (AAUW); secretary of the regional AAUW organization; president of the Missouri AAUW; member of the Spiva Art Center, the Joplin YWCA, Women of Rotary, Delta Kappa Gamma Sorority, and the Business and Professional Women's Club. Mrs. Hoover received an international grant in her honor from the Joplin AAUW, recognition for thirty-three years of service in the Business and Professional Women's Club, and the Rex Plumbum Award from the Joplin Historical Society for outstanding service in preserving the history of Joplin and its surrounding area. She was the editor/publisher of Tales About Joplin—Short and Tall *by Evelyn Milligan Jones.*

Her determination to preserve the history of this area led to the establishment of the Dorothea B. Hoover Historical Museum in Schifferdecker Park. Dorothea B. Hoover died in 1972. From the Dorothea B. Hoover Historical Museum

The Joplin Historical Society was chartered on June 27, 1966. One of its first goals was the establishment of a historical museum to comple- ment the city-owned Tri-State Miner- al Museum. In May 1976 the Dorothea B. Hoover Historical Museum was opened in Schiffer- decker Park. This photograph shows the mineral museum on the left and the historical museum on the right. Photograph by Jim Mueller

More than 134,000 airline passengers passed through the boarding and departure gates of the Joplin Municipal Airport in 1978, and that number was expected to increase. Improvements planned for the near future will cost more than $2.7 million dollars. Photograph by Jim Mueller; courtesy of the Joplin Chamber of Commerce

The modern St. John's Medical Center at 2727 McClelland Boulevard is quite different in appearance from the original hospital. Its aims and purposes are still the same, even though patient care and diagnostic services now number seventy-four and range from anesthesiology to x-ray. Courtesy of St. John's Medical Center

Joplin had a town crier for its celebration of the United States Bicentennial in 1976. Joe Blanchard is shown in full costume for his role in the festivities. Courtesy of Joe Blanchard

Joplin took part in the United States Bicentennial celebration with a party which included this birthday cake displayed on March 28, 1976. The cake was baked and decorated by Mrs. George Heinbein. Courtesy of Helen Knight Chickering

153

The Bicentennial celebration was dampened by the more than ten inches of rain which fell on July 3, 1976. Willow Branch, which normally flows unnoticed under Main, inundated the downtown area with three to four feet of water, causing millions of dollars worth of damage. The two photographs taken at Fifth and Main show the center of town before and after the water receded. The automobile was washed into Joplin Creek beside Plaza Lanes at Eastmoreland Plaza. From the postcard collection of Ron Mosbaugh

Atlas Power Company manufactures commerical explosives and nitrogen fertilizers. Located east of Joplin, the plant employs more than 500 people. Now a subsidiary of Tyler Corporation of Dallas, the Atlas plant was established in 1912. Photograph by Jim Mueller; from the Joplin Chamber of Commerce

This aerial view of the $8 million campus of the Ozark Bible College on North Main shows part of the 130-acre tract the college now occupies. From an enrollment of only 20 students in 1944, the college has become the largest of nearly forty facilities among the Christian churches and the Churches of Christ worldwide. The college offers ten degrees and enrolls more than 600 students each semester. Courtesy of Ozark Bible College

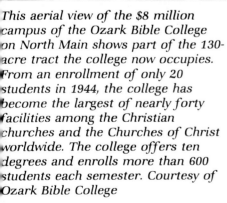

This aerial view shows the ninety-eight-bed Oak Hill Osteopathic Hospital at Thirty-Fourth and Indiana. Courtesy of Oak Hill Osteopathic Hospital

155

John Beal has appeared in more than 200 roles on Broadway, in films, and on radio and television. Born James Alexander Bliedung in Joplin on August 13, 1909, he was the son of Edmund Bliedung, one of the founders of Christman's Department Store. His sister, Dorothea, became an important force in Joplin's cultural life. Beal graduated from Joplin High School in 1926, already showing promise in the fields of acting and art. After he received a B. S. from the University of Pennsylvania's Wharton School of Finance and Commerce in 1930, he studied at the Art Students' League in New York and worked at the Hedgerow Theater in Moylan, Pennsylvania. Beal starred in Mask and Wig productions at college and had his first speaking part in No More Frontier in 1931. His successful film career included more than sixty films such as The Little Minister, Les Miserables, My Six Convicts, Ten Who Dared, The Sound and the Fury, Edge of Darkness and Key Witness. Theater roles include Liberty Jones, The Teahouse of the August Moon, The Voice of the Turtle, and Long Day's Journey Into Night. Television appearances have included The Adams Chronicles, The Waltons, Kojak, The Streets of San Francisco, The Blue Knight, Family, and Barnaby Jones. Brooks Atkinson, critic for the New York Times, said, "John Beal is one of the best actors in our theatre." Beal is also an accomplished artist and a portrait painter of considerable fame. He is married to actress Helen Craig, and they have two daughters, Tita and Tandy. Courtesy of John Beal

Tri-State Motor Transit Company was incorporated in 1931 to transport explosives within Missouri, Kansas, and Oklahoma. Today it ranks among the top 100 freight transportation companies in dollar volume operating in America. The company specializes in transportation of heavy and bulky items, various types of explosives, nuclear and radioactive materials, aerospace articles, pipeline equipment, and more than 100 specific commodities. The company's corporate headquarters are in Joplin. From the Joplin Chamber of Commerce

The Empire District Electric Company was established in 1909, although its predecessor companies date back to 1887. With more than 96,000 customers in the tri-state area, it employs more than 500 people. This photograph shows the generating plant on Spring River west of Joplin in Riverton, Kansas. From the Joplin Chamber of Commerce

The Joplin Globe has been a vital part of the community since it was founded on August 9, 1896, by three printers who championed the cause of William Jennings Bryan in the presidential campaign. The town was predominately Democratic at the time, and the paper became very popular. Gilbert Barbee, mining operator, builder, and colorful Democratic politician, gained controlling interest around the turn of the century and built a two-story brick building to house the Globe at Fourth and Virginia. In 1910, A. H. Rogers, builder of an interurban streetcar system linking Joplin with district mining towns, purchased controlling interest in the Globe. The Joplin News Herald was acquired by the Joplin Globe in 1919. Other papers, such as the Joplin American and the Tribune have disappeared from the scene. The Joplin Globe became a division of Ottaway News, Inc., a subsidiary of Dow Jones, Inc., on November 1, 1976. The Globe has expanded its operation several times over the years, including a one million-dollar expansion project which was completed in 1973, but is still located at Fourth and Virginia. This photograph was taken from the corner of Fourth and Main and shows the Spiva Park in the foreground. From the Joplin Chamber of Commerce

Eagle-Picher Industries, Inc., was formed by a merger in 1916 of The Eagle White Lead Company and the Picher Lead Company, with Oliver Picher as president. Until the 1940s, Eagle-Picher remained principally a lead and zinc mining and processing company. As a result of a planned diversification program, the company now includes industrial, machinery, and automotive groups which manufacture germanium for the electronics industry, fertilizer, insulation, batteries of all types, molded plastic parts, aluminum castings, earthmoving equipment, molded rubber products, and high purity boron isotopes for the nuclear industry. With net sales in 1978 of more than $525 million Eagle-Picher ranks in the top thirty percent of this country's largest manufacturing companies in the rate of return on common equity. This photograph shows the Joplin complex at C and Porter. A lead smelter and pigment plant in 1887, the complex now produces sophisticated special-purpose batteries for aerospace and defense applications as well as lead and zinc chemicals and industrial insulations. From the Joplin Chamber of Commerce

The Joplin Municipal Building at 303 East Third houses city offices, the fire and police departments, and civil defense headquarters for Joplin. The city employs more than 350 people in these and other departments. Since 1954 when a new city charter was adopted providing for the council-manager form of government, a city manager has been hired by the nine elected city council members to serve as administrative head of the city. The city budget for 1979-80 was almost $11.5 million. Photography by Jim Mueller; from the Joplin Chamber of Commerce

*Joplin Memorial High School (left) at
300 West Eighth and Parkwood High
School (right) at Twentieth and
Indiana now serve the secondary
needs of the Joplin R-8 School
District. The school district covers
approximately seventy square miles
in Jasper and Newton counties and
enrolls about 8,000 students.
Photographs by Jim Mueller*

The Joplin Water Works at Twenty-first between Picher and Empire was founded in 1881 by Patrick Murphy and Oliver Picher of Joplin and David B. Sears of Rock Island, Illinois. It has been owned since 1889 by the American Water Works Company. Serving about 16,200 customers, the company processed and pumped over 9 million gallons of water per day in 1978. A new 1 million-gallon ground storage tank has recently been completed, bringing water storage capacity of 3.5 million gallons. From the Joplin Chamber of Commerce

Agriculture in the tri-state area is quite diversified. Area farming is dominated by family operations, with grain and livestock production and sales the dominating factors in Jasper County. Other crops in the area include soybeans, corn, milo, poultry and eggs, black walnuts, and pecans. Missouri pastures were upgraded several years ago with the introduction of fescue. A strong interest in the production of gasohol has resulted from current fuel shortages. Specialty crops ranging from popcorn to contract grape production have grown rapidly in the district. The 1978 sales receipts at the Joplin stockyards exceeded $50 million. Photograph by Jim Mueller; from the Joplin Chamber of Commerce

Dennis Weaver was born in 1925 and brought up in Joplin. Weaver was an outstanding athlete while attending public schools and the Joplin Junior College. He enlisted in the Navy Air Force and was a member of the Navy's track and field squad. After his discharge he attended the University of Oklahoma where he led his college squad to the national championships in track and field and personally qualified for the U. S. Olympic trials in the decathlon in 1948. He appeared in several Broadway productions including Come Back, Little Sheba and Steetcar Named Desire. He developed the role of Chester in Gunsmoke on television, and in 1959 won an Emmy Award for best supporting actor in a series; he continued in this role for nine years. Weaver's McCloud series ran from 1970 to 1977, providing him with an opportunity to exercise his many-sided acting talents. His movie credits include Horizons West, Dragnet, The Bridges at Toko Ri, Touch of Evil, and The Gallant Hours. Other television credits include Gentle Ben, and The Gallant Hours. Other television credits include Gentle Ben, The Forgotten Man, The Great Man's Whiskers, and Intimate Strangers. Weaver was president of the Screen Actors' Guild 1973-75. He married Gerry Stowell in 1945, and they have three sons. Active in community affairs, they were named "Family of the Year" by their neighbors. Weaver was guest speaker at a fund-raising banquet in 1967 that raised one million dollars for Freeman Hospital. Courtesy of Dennis Weaver

Dennis Weaver uses a teenager's back for a desk as he signs autographs during "Dennis Weaver Day" in October 1967. It was the closing day of Joplin's first annual Fall Festival of the Arts. The road leading toward Joplin Municipal Airport was named Dennis Weaver Boulevard in his honor. Photograph by Charles Snow

163

The Eastmoreland Plaza Shopping Center at Seventh and Illinois was still under construction when this photograph was taken in 1955. It now houses thirty-five businesses with an additional nineteen in the Mart Plaza which was recently completed next to Plaza Lanes. Historic Joplin Creek is shown in the right foreground. From the Joplin Chamber of Commerce

The largest shopping center in the Joplin area is Northpark Mall, located at 101 Range Line near the intersection of U. S. 66 and U. S. 71. Built on a sixty-two acre tract, the mall has seventy-four shops ranging from full-line department stores to specialty shops and food service facilities. Major expansion plans have recently been unveiled. A fact sheet distributed by the Northpark Mall shows that there are 355,000 people within a thirty-five mile radius. Courtesy of the Northpark Mall

Joplin continues to grow and build. This photograph shows The Park, a new apartment house development at Seventeenth and Campbell Parkway. More than 1,200 apartment units have been developed in Joplin in the past decade. Photograph by Jim Mueller; from the Joplin Chamber of Commerce

Among the features of the Tri-State Mineral Museum in Schifferdecker Park are these handcrafted replicas of early mining operations. Photographs by Kay Kirkman

The Joplin Little Theatre is located beside Schifferdecker Park at First and Adams. Established in the 1930s, the theatre provides an opportunity for area residents to act and work in the production of several plays each year. Photograph by Kay Kirkman

168

Site of
FIRST DISCOVERY OF LEAD IN JOPLIN
ABOUT 1849

FIRST SHAFT SUNK
WHERE SLAVE BOY HAD DUG
FOR WORMS, BUT ALL MINING
CLOSED DURING CIVIL WAR
AND GUERRILLA WARFARE
AFTER IT WHEN E.R.MOFFET
AND JOHN B.SERGEANT'S
"DISCOVERY SHAFT" PROVED A BONANZA
MINERS FROM ALL OVER THE WORLD
CAME. JAN.1871. 20 PROSPECTORS
WORKING UP & DOWN JOPLIN CREEK
VALLEY. BY JUNE VALLEY FILLED WITH
BOX HOUSES & TENTS.AUG.500 MINERS
& "JOPLIN CAMP" WAS ON IT'S WAY.

In the 1960s the Joplin Historical Society established the Joplin Historical Trail, which includes more than twenty points of interest, such as the site of the first mine shaft sunk in the Joplin area. A. H. Rogers, whose residence is marked on the trail, was an 1878 Harvard graduate from Iowa. In 1879 he organized the Twin Cities Street Railway Company which connected Webb City and Carterville and which later became the Southwest Missouri Railroad, connecting mining areas in Missouri, Kansas, and Oklahoma. Rogers built a streetcar service in Joplin in 1893, operated a wholesale grocery company, financed the Joplin American newspaper in 1905, and purchased controlling interest in the Joplin Globe in 1910. Photographs by Kay Kirkman

The Joplin Municipal Golf Course at Schifferdecker Park remains a popular recreational spot for Joplinites. From the Joplin Chamber of Commerce

169

8
Chapter

Then and Now

172

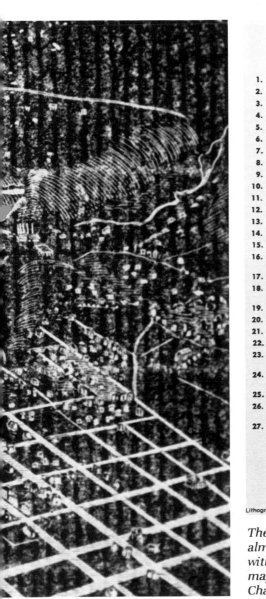

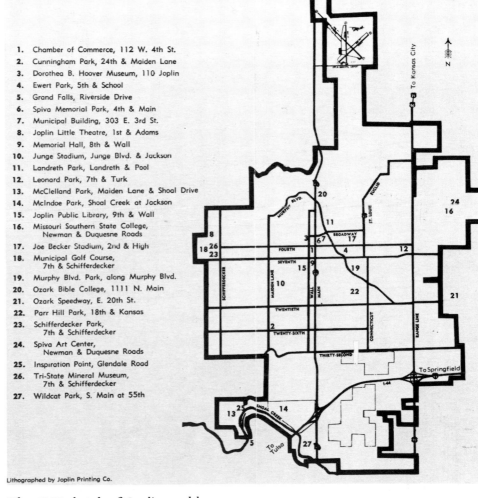

1. Chamber of Commerce, 112 W. 4th St.
2. Cunningham Park, 24th & Maiden Lane
3. Dorothea B. Hoover Museum, 110 Joplin
4. Ewert Park, 5th & School
5. Grand Falls, Riverside Drive
6. Spiva Memorial Park, 4th & Main
7. Municipal Building, 303 E. 3rd St.
8. Joplin Little Theatre, 1st & Adams
9. Memorial Hall, 8th & Wall
10. Junge Stadium, Junge Blvd. & Jackson
11. Landreth Park, Landreth & Pool
12. Leonard Park, 7th & Turk
13. McClelland Park, Maiden Lane & Shoal Drive
14. McIndoe Park, Shoal Creek at Jackson
15. Joplin Public Library, 9th & Wall
16. Missouri Southern State College,
    Newman & Duquesne Roads
17. Joe Becker Stadium, 2nd & High
18. Municipal Golf Course,
    7th & Schifferdecker
19. Murphy Blvd. Park, along Murphy Blvd.
20. Ozark Bible College, 1111 N. Main
21. Ozark Speedway, E. 20th St.
22. Parr Hill Park, 18th & Kansas
23. Schifferdecker Park,
    7th & Schifferdecker
24. Spiva Art Center,
    Newman & Duquesne Roads
25. Inspiration Point, Glendale Road
26. Tri-State Mineral Museum,
    7th & Schifferdecker
27. Wildcat Park, S. Main at 55th

Lithographed by Joplin Printing Co.

*The 1887 sketch of Joplin could
almost fit in the tiny section marked
with the number one on the outline
map of Joplin today. From the Joplin
Chamber of Commerce*

Downtown Joplin in the 1890s, around 1912, and in the 1970s. Note that the 1912 photograph is mislabeled; it was actually taken from Seventh Street looking north. From the Joplin Chamber of Commerce

The first graduates from St. John's School of Nursing in 1905, and the first graduates of St. John's School of Radiologic Technology in 1973. St. John's graduated 429 nurses between 1905 and 1961 when the school of nursing was closed. From St. John's Medical Center

Elephants lead the parade in this 1880 photograph which shows Joplin's Main Street from Second to Fourth. From the Joplin Chamber of Commerce

"Tip-Top Bread, the Staff of Life, 100% Pure" proclaims this sign on the Junge Baking Company wagon decorated for a parade circa-1905. From Alberta Junge York

This St. John's Hospital float reflected patriotic spirit in the 1920s. From St. John's Medical Center

This group of young patriots paraded in 1924. The photograph was taken looking south on Joplin from Fifth. From the Joplin Chamber of Commerce

Joplin youngsters celebrate the American Bicentennial with a bicycle parade in 1976. Photograph by Jim Mueller; from the Joplin Chamber of Commerce

The Joplin Fiesta Parade of 1941. From Baird Studios

The Jasper County Courthouse for the Western Division was built in 1894 on the southeast corner of Seventh and Virginia. Today's modern courthouse is located at Sixth and Pearl. Courthouse of 1894 from the postcard collection of Ron Mosbaugh; 1976 courthouse photographed by Jim Mueller

Wig Hill was the name given to the residence of John C. Cox, founder of Joplin. Located at 615 Persimmon, the house is owned today by Mr. and Mrs. Ronald C. Apfel. Mrs. Apfel is the great-granddaughter of Cox. The brick house, whose foundation was started before the Civil War, was completed around 1866-67. Most of Cox's original frame buildings were burned during the Civil War. Only the old granary, which may also have been used as a smoke house and kitchen, is still standing. These views show Wig Hill in the 1880s and the 1970s. From the Joplin Chamber of Commerce

THE CONNOR
by Elizabeth Nolan Wilson
O symbol of a leisured time, of elegance and grace,
O rendezvous for celebrants, where Titans set the pace.
What memories of glories past illuminate your halls,
Of dancers, formally attired, those wonderous Programme Balls!
The magic rhythmic melodies the music masters made,
The mellow, glowing ambiance. The big bands—how they played!
If ghosts could talk!
And then you stood abandoned and alone,
Reduced by so-called progress to nine cold floors of stone,
Your marble stairs, rotunda, forgotten by your town
Like someone's poor relation in tattered evening gown.
Besieged by taxes, changing times, neglect and wind and rain,
You stood erect, aloof and tall, and tried to hide the pain.
No detonator, not for you as loomed the fated knell—
You bowed, disdainful, proud throughout, and broken-hearted,
Fell.

This photograph was taken on the evening of Saturday, November 11, 1978, when workmen were digging through the rubble in a frantic search for the three men who were buried when the Connor Hotel suddenly collapsed while being rigged for demolition. Only one man survived. Photograph by Charles Snow.

Joplin Memorial Hall was dedicated "In Memory of Our National Defenders" in 1924. Located at Eighth and Joplin, it is shown here prior to renovation in 1976. The interior photograph shows the renovated civic center. From the Joplin Chamber of Commerce

Over the years, identities of people and places often become confused. The bar shown in this early picture is identified as the House of Lords, yet it seems far too plain for the opulence described by such visitors as Thomas Hart Benton. On the other hand, Frona Norman stands beside a painting which she acquired when the House of Lords closed in 1919 and which fits the description of the decor of that famous bar; yet many argue that the painting never actually hung in the House of Lords. Perhaps no verifiable pictures of the interior of the House of Lords will ever be found, and it will remain a richly embroidered tapestry of memory. "House of Lords Bar" from the postcard collection of Ron Mosbaugh; photograph of Frona Norman by Charles Snow

The First Presbyterian Church and parsonage on the northeast corner of Sixth and Pearl was completed at a cost of $25,000 in 1902. Designed by A. C. Michaelis in the style of a Grecian temple with elliptical ceilings and a gallery overlooking the auditorium, this structure burned in the 1920s. From the Dorothea B. Hoover Historical Museum

The sanctuary of the First Presbyterian Church at Fifth and Pearl was completed in 1973, one hundred years after the church was organized in Joplin. This was the third church building erected by the Presbyterian congregation. Courtesy of the First Presbyterian Church

LOVERS' TUB &
SCHIFFERDECK
J

LOVERS' TUB &
SCHIFFERDECK
JC

Y' DAZER RIDES
LECTRIC PARK.
, MO.

Schifferdecker Park is still a favorite gathering place for people from the Joplin area. Shelter houses provide meeting places for family reunions, company picnics, and simple get-togethers. Children can climb over an early railroad car, a truck, or an airplane, or they can scramble into a model rocket for a quick trip down the slippery slide. The golf course, swimming pool, museums, and tennis courts are as appealing to today's residents as the Schifferdecker Electric Park was to citizens of the early 1900s. Photographs by Kay Kirkman

Acknowledgments

It would be impossible to list all those who have helped us research the history of Joplin as well as locate and identify the photographs used in this book. We would like to thank Jim Mueller and Charles Snow, whose photographic skills turned yellowed fragments of paper into usable prints. We appreciate the encouragement and support of our families, Sherrie Stinnett, Bill Kirkman, and Mildred Williams, as well as the help of Kathleen, Pete, and Paul Kirkman, who spent many research hours in libraries, newspaper offices, and at the State Historical Society in Columbia, Missouri. We also want to specially thank the following:

Helen and Chester Chickering
Alma Doan
Mr. and Mrs. Gale Graham
Dorothea B. Hoover Historical Museum
Joplin Chamber of Commerce
Joplin Historical Society
Bob Phillips
Bruce Quisenberry

Everett Ritchie
Hilda Satterlee
State Historical Society of Missouri
Rolla Stephens
Tri-State Mineral Museum
William C. Troutman III
Mary Curtis Warten
Betty Nolan Wilson

Kay Kirkman has earned degrees in journalism and creative writing. She taught adult continuing education creative writing courses at Missouri Southern State College. She is past president of the Joplin Writers' Guild, a member of the Missouri Writers' Guild and the National Writers' Club. Kirkman is currently enrolled in a master's degree program in creative writing. She has had numerous articles published and is under contract for two more non-fiction books.

A third generation Joplin native, Roger Stinnett is a member of the Joplin Historical Society, Joplin Genealogical Society and the State Historical Society of Missouri.

An instructor of Social Studies at North Junior High, Reverend Stinnett is also Pastor of St. Michael and All Angels' Reformed Episcopal Church.

Bibliography

Beatty, C. E., and James F. Snow. *Joplin, Missouri—Mining and Industrial Interests.* Kansas City: Hudson-Kimberly Publishing, 1890.

Conard, Howard L., ed. *Encyclopedia of the History of Missouri.* New York: Southern History, 1901.

Igenthron, Elmo. *Indians of the Ozark Plateau.* Point Lookout, MO: School of the Ozarks Press, 1970.

Joplin, Missouri—The City That "Jack" Built. N.p.: Means Moore, 1902

Joplin, Missouri—The City of Wealth, Industry and Opportunity. Joplin: Commercial Club, 1913.

Livingston, Joel T. *A History of Jasper County, Missouri, and Its People.* Chicago: Lewis Publishing, 1912.

Meyer, Duane. *The Heritage of Missouri—A History.* Hazelwood, MO: State Publishing, 1970.

The Mines and the Miners. Writ. and dir. Bob Phillips. KODE-TV, 1972.

North, F. A., ed. *The History of Jasper County Missouri.* Des Moines, IA: Mills, 1883.

Shaner, Dolph. *The Story of Joplin.* New York: Stratford House, 1948.

Warten, Mary Curtis, ed. *Thomas Hart Benton: A Personal Commemorative.* Kansas City: Burd and Fletcher, 1973.